STILL SMALL VOICE

POEMS ON MY LIFE AND MY LORD

by
Betty Holt

I want to express my gratitude to my sons, Stephen and Daniel, and my daughter, Esther, for their help in getting this book published.

Still Small Voice: Poems On My Life and My Lord
Copyright © 2020 Elizabeth J. Holt
All rights reserved.

Except otherwise stated, all Scripture taken from the New King James Version®.
Copyright © 1982 by Thomas Nelson.

Contents

ABOUT THE AUTHOR

Betty Holt was born in Chicago, Illinois. At the age of 8, she became convicted of the sin in her life and asked the Lord Jesus Christ to forgive her and make her clean. At the age of 14, she surrendered her life wholly to God, to serve Him whenever, wherever and however He should direct.

As a young adult, in 1960, Betty graduated from the Moody Bible Institute and joined a group of fellow students for evangelistic work in Mexico throughout that summer. This work eventually developed into the mission organisation known as 'Operation Mobilisation' (OM). After being involved with this mission for ten years across Europe, Betty married Peter Holt whilst living in Belgium, and had four children there.

In 1981 the family moved to Cornwall, in England, where they stayed for around 18 years. After that, they moved around England, living in Sheffield, Canterbury and then Farnborough in Hampshire. More recently Betty has moved northwards to Northamptonshire in order to be near her eldest son and his family. The poem *It Goes With The Silver Hair* gives a hint as to her current stage in life as well as adding a touch of humour.

INTRODUCTION

I started writing poetry as a child, but the little ditties I included with the Christmas presents I gave to my family members are not included here as they sadly no longer exist. The ones that I wrote as a young, single adult are indicated by being dated before 31 July 1971, the date of my marriage. There was then a gap in my poetry writing while I was caring for our family of four children. In later years, I was again able to take up the pen and express my deepest thoughts, and some superficial ones, in poetry.

The title *Still, Small Voice* comes from the thought that when God speaks it is often not with a megaphone but in a still, quiet voice – to hear Him you may need to pause, lean-in and listen. I pray that as you read these poems you also will also hear His voice.

All of the poems contained in this volume are expressions of my heart-felt feelings about life's experiences and about my deep faith in God. It is sent out with the prayer that many will be blessed through reading them, and that God will be glorified.

Betty Holt
July 2020

PRAYER

THANK YOU LORD

Thank You Lord for keeping me in the hollow of Your hand.
Thank You for giving me grace, every trial to withstand.
Thank You for being near me each day,
Helping me, even when I cannot pray.

15 June 2010

PLEASE GUIDE ME, LORD

Please guide me, Lord, throughout today,
In all I do, in all I say;
May I glorify You in every way.

May I, in every passing day
Seek only to walk Your way;
And help those who might go astray.

You have made straight paths for all
Who in their need upon You call;
Upheld by You, they shall not fall.

Please keep me, Lord, throughout this night;
May I wake up to the morning light
To serve You, Lord, with all my might.

19 January 2018

STOP!

Just stop for a minute to kneel and pray,
Even when tired and full of dismay.
Prayer will prepare you another day to start.
Even if from loved-ones far apart.

When you come to the day in the middle of the week,
Join with other saints your prayers to speak.
Pray for all your friends and neighbours,
Pray for all those in God's labours.

Week after week, can you say,
"I have stopped every day to kneel and pray"?
Time is fleeting and will soon pass away.
Won't you stop just now to kneel and pray?

April 12 1958

All of us face difficulties, disappointments and, sometimes, persecution. God allows these things, and desires to use them to purify us in one way or another. I Peter 1:7 says, "That the genuineness of your faith, being much more precious than gold that perishes, though it is tested by fire, may be found to praise, honour, and glory at the revelation of Jesus Christ."

NOT I, BUT CHRIST

I want to press on to know the Lord,
To follow Him and fully obey His Word.
Many and sad have my failures been;
All along I prayed that Jesus would be seen.

"Others hinder me" I'd oft complain;
But when I meet my Saviour, I'll bear the blame.
Gold tried in the fire comes out pure;
Has the fire done this in me? I'm not sure.

Have my works been wood, hay and stubble?
Will there be any reward for my trouble?
Please grant me the soul-winner's crown
To lay at Your feet when in worship I bow down.

Lord, my heart's desire is You to serve,
The lost and wayward from punishment to swerve,
That they might know You, th'eternal Lord,
The living, dying and resurrected Word.

6 January 1998

MY PRAYERS FOR OTHERS

My prayers for others are of no avail
If, in prayer I don't prevail;
I must have God's victory,
If the same in them I'd see.

Lord, how long I've stumbled on
When I ought to rise and run!
How long revelled in earth-bound desire,
When Thou dost long to take me higher.

Restore to me Thy joy, dear Lord;
Speak clearly through Thy holy Word.
As my thoughts to Thee I render,
Let me see Thee in Thy splendour.

7 November 1990

MISSION

Thinking of Psalm 126:5 – 6. "Those who sow in tears shall reap in joy. He who continually goes forth weeping, bearing seed for sowing, shall doubtless come again with rejoicing, bringing his sheaves with him."

I SOW IN TEARS

Men lost in darkness, sin and despair;
No hope of cleansing or glory there.
Lord, send me out, Thy love to share,
Let nought of my sin Thy work impair.

They trample Your holy name in dust,
Afraid Your wonderful love to trust.
They choose to live according to lust,
And lay up riches which will rust.

If only now Your love they'd know –
Believe You truly love them so!
Oh, send me forth, Your seed to sow,
And send me weeping as I go.

7 May 1966

PRIORITIES

Are we so busy feeding the over-fed
That we have no time to help the spiritually dead
To hear the way of eternal life?

Are we going in circles like a lark,
Instead of "pressing on toward the mark",
Caught up in our busy, busy life?

In what, then, do we take delight?
In deeds of darkness, or of the light?
Between the two, there's always strife.

So let us choose to follow Him,
Dying to self, forsaking sin;
Living for Him, who is our life.

20 January 2018

In the autumn of 1963 I joined the OM office team in Atherton, Lancashire, England. One of the men who should have been there with us was, along with another brother, imprisoned in Yugoslavia for distributing Christian literature. This was still under the Communist era, when such activity was forbidden. A third brother was being held elsewhere for the same reason. Naturally we were concerned for their well-being, and daily prayed fervently for their release. This poem was written during that time.

SAFE IN THE HOLLOW OF HIS HAND

Safe the hollow of His hand,
Is where God's children always stand;
Tempted, tried and laden with care;
There's no need to worry there.
We're safe in the hollow of His hand.

Though far off in a heathen land,
Where God's name is loved by no man;
Though bound in jail or prison drear,
No word of home his heart to cheer,
Mark's safe in the hollow of His hand.

The whereabouts of Tony and Pete,
'Unknown to us' we oft repeat;
But God knows where our brothers are,
And He tells us to never fear.
They, too, are safe in the hollow of His hand.

11 September 1965

Praise be to God! They were all later released, and returned home safe and sound.

From October 1961 to June 1962, I worked with an OM travelling team throughout Austria and Germany. We did door-to-door evangelism during the day, Mondays to Fridays, and met with church youth groups evenings and weekends. Our goal was to challenge and encourage other Christian young people to join with us during the summer of 1962 in order to spread God's Word more widely in cities throughout Europe.

In one of those churches, a young man said to me in German, "You know what OM means? I said, "Yes, Operation Mobilisation." He replied, "No, it means Ohne Mich!" Which means 'without me.' His words stuck in my mind; he could see the need but was unwilling to be a part of the solution. His comments brought me to write this poem.

OM MEANS: WITHOUT ME ... OR DOES IT?

Without me they will not hear,
Many people live in fear.
Can I say: "I'm staying here?"

Jesus says: "Go forth,
Bring the Word to everyone.
Do you love me? Then go!"

Lord, give me Your love,
I must go and bring them in.
Without me it cannot be.

OM HEISST: OHNE MICH ... ODER?

Ohne mich hören sie nicht,
Viele Menschen haben kein Licht.
Kann ich sagen: „ich gehe nicht?"

Jezus saget: „Gehe hin,
Bringe das Wort den Einzelnen;
Liebst du mich? So gehe hin."

Schenke mir, Herr, Liebe Dein,
Ich muss gehen und sie bringen herein.
Ohne mich kann es nicht sein!

1963

REFLECTIONS ON THE CROSS

Sometimes, by the end of a Communion service my mind and heart are overwhelmed with worship, resulting in a poem. The following poems are a few of those reflections.

"And as they were eating, Jesus took bread, blessed and broke it, and gave it to the disciples and said, "Take, eat; this is My body." Then He took the cup, and gave thanks, and gave it to them, saying, "Drink from it, all of you. For this is My blood of the new covenant, which is shed for many for the remission of sins. But I say to you, I will not drink of this fruit of the vine from now on until that day when I drink it new with you in My Father's kingdom." Matthew 26:26 – 29.

REMEMBER ME

Thank You for bearing my sins upon the tree;
Thank You for giving me life and liberty.
Oh, how sweet it is to remember Thee!

Remember me, is what our Saviour said,
Before God's wrath came down upon His head.
Remember Him, who is no longer dead.

20 May 2012

HOW CAN I PRAISE MY LORD ENOUGH?

Those gentle hands with nails were torn,
Upon His head, that crown of thorn;
The Lamb of God bad men did scorn.
How can I praise my Lord enough?

How precious is the sinless blood
That cleanses me and sets me free
And makes me His for eternity!
How can I praise my Lord enough?

The perfect Man was crucified;
Was sorely beaten ere He died.
"It is finished" He loudly cried.
How can I praise my Lord enough?

My every stain He took away;
They'll not be thought of on That Day,
No matter what the accusers say.
How can I praise my Lord enough?

13 February 2011

THE SHEPHERD GAVE HIS LIFE FOR HIS SHEEP

The Shepherd gave His life for His sheep;
He truly did, He did not sleep.
In this, He was the Lamb of God,
Upon whom fell the judgement rod.

As Priest, Himself He sacrificed;
God's holiness was satisfied.
As Priest, He lives and for us prays.
One day, He'll judge all of man's ways.

Yes, He, who was the perfect One
Took all our sins and did atone,
That we might be as pure as He,
And live throughout eternity.

27 May 2018

WONDERFUL EXCHANGES

On the cross Christ took my death – and gave me His life;
He took my punishment – and promised me a reward;
He took my sorrows – and gave me His joy.
He took my weakness – and gave strength without alloy.
For my fears, He gave me peace;
From my bondage, sweet release.
He replaced my darkness with His light;
Removed my blindness, gave me sight.
Christ, the Righteous Branch cut down –
Now He's the Vine, and we the branches.

15 May 2010

JUDAS, THE TRAITOR

Now Judas was a disciple of Christ, but he was a greedy man;
Responsible for the disciples' purse, He sometimes dipped his hand.
And when he saw how good perfume on Jesus' feet was poured,
He said, "Why make such a waste? That could have fed the poor."
That could have fed the poor.

An idea on how to get more cash was the devil's wicked plan.
Judas went to the temple and told the priests, "I'll lead you to your man."
And as the Saviour was in the Garden, Judas greeted Him with a kiss,
And said, "This is the One you're looking for. His friendship I won't miss."
His friendship I won't miss.

But when he saw that Jesus was condemned to die,
Judas felt a pang of guilt, and hurried out, but not to cry.
He should have asked our Saviour, his treason to forgive;
Instead, he decided that he could no longer live.
Judas hanged himself – in shame he could not live.

The other disciples were faithful and true,
They lived to serve Jesus, some were martyred, too.
Knowing that in Heaven we have a better place
When we shall see our Saviour's face.
What joy, when we shall see His face!

25 January 2018

"Then Jesus said to the twelve, do you also want to go away? Then Simon Peter answered him, Lord, to whom shall we go? You have the words of eternal life." John 6:67 – 68.

WILL YOU ALSO GO AWAY?

Crowds followed Jesus because they'd been fed,
He'd healed the sick and raised the dead.
But when the Son of Man said,
"Take up your cross and follow Me,"
They turned and fled.

His disciples said, "We'll never leave You,
To our Master we'll be true."
But when soldiers to arrest Him
Came, they were afraid, and so, too,
They turned and fled.

He bled for my sins on Calvary's cross.
When trials come to burn my dross,
May I say, "Lord, all else is loss;"
To whom else should Your saved ones go?
Let us to Him flee.

2 November 1998

FROM SORROW COMES JOY

With crown of thorns pressed on His head,
His body broken, His blood was shed,
The soldiers jeered; our Lord was dead.

Why did He have to suffer so,
And hang on a cross of shame and woe?
It was because He loves us so.

But there the story did not end:
Up from the grave He did ascend!
Now He our broken lives can mend.

He sent the Comforter to all
Who for salvation on Him call.
Thus, out of sorrow joy can flow.

26 February 2017

OUR SAVIOUR

Whoever came to Him in need,
Or for another one to plead,
To each He did give earnest heed
And showed that His is love indeed.
How loving is our Saviour!

In agony, He prayed alone:
"Yet not my will, but Thine be done."
His back was striped; His face was torn;
He died that we might be reborn.
How faithful is our Saviour!

Oh, how precious is His blood
That became a cleansing flood,
Washing us clean and making good
We who have now understood –
How precious is our Saviour!

Oh Lord, our God, our Creator,
We worship You, our great Saviour.
You laid Your life on God's altar,
And rose again, the great Victor.
How mighty is our Saviour!

8 July 2012

AS YOU WERE BROKEN FOR ME

As You were broken for me,
Let me be broken for Thee;
Thy blood was shed for sin,
Oh, keep me pure within.

You gave Yourself to set me free.
Now let me Your channel be
Through which to pour Your life and power,
Every day and fleeting hour.

Your perfect work of Calvary,
Please perfect each day in me.

1966

THANK YOU LORD FOR CALVARY

Thank You Lord for Calvary,
Thanks for the blood that cleanses me,
Thanks for the cross that sets me free,
Thanks for all eternity.

August 1983

"Whom have I in heaven but You? And there is none upon earth that I desire besides You."
Psalm 73:25

TO YOU I OWE MY LIFE

To You I owe my life, and give it willingly;
Because You gave Yourself in dying on a tree.

Your love, my Lord, surpasses the love of any man.
So gladly I will serve You the very best I can.

Not only did You save me, You guide me day by day;
You answer every problem that comes along my way.

"No, I will never leave you," is what Your promise said;
And in the end, You will raise me up from among the dead.

December 2016

"If I regard iniquity in my heart, the Lord will not hear me." Psalm 66:18.

I don't remember why I wrote this one in Spanish. It might just be that the words popped into my head in that language. Here's the nearest to poetic translation I can do and the Spanish version is below.

YOUR EAR DID NOT HEAR ME

Your ear did not hear me
When I did not believe in Thee.
I shortened your hand,
While my sin separated me from Thee.

In spite of this, you loved me,
And forgave me of my sin,
Because now I believe:
I trust in Your beloved Son.

His death and resurrection
Are a victorious action,
Which provides eternal life
To everyone who believes.

Though I am a poor disciple,
Yet You answer my prayers;
In spite of my mistakes,
You deliver me from my fears.

Now I await Your return
From the heavens in glory,
When every eye shall see You,
And every tongue confess You.

10 May 2006

"Si yo en mi corazòn hubiera visto iniquidad, el Señor no me hubiera escuchado:" Salmo 66:18. Biblia de Jerusalén (1975)

TU OREJA NO ME OÍA

Tu oreja no me oía,
Cuando en Tu nombre yo no creía.
Tu mano yo te cortaba
Mientras mi pecado de Ti me separaba.

A pesar de esto, me amas,
Y de mi pecado perdonas
Porque ahora creo;
En Tu Hijo bien amado confío.

Su muerte y resurrección
Es una victoriosa acción,
Que provee la vida eterna
Para cada persona que crea.

Aunque soy una pobre discípula,
Mis oraciones me contestas.
A pesar de mis errores,
Me libras de todos temores.

Ahora espero Tu venida
De los cielos en la gloria,
Cuando todo ojo te verá,
Y cada lengua te confesará.

10 Mayo 2006

WHEN YOU SEEK THE SAVIOUR'S FACE

When you seek the Saviour's face,
All your sins He will erase
From the books He keeps above,
For He has the greatest love
Ever known by the human race.

February 1957

GOD'S VOICE

God's powerful voice made the heavens and the earth;
He said: Let there be light, water, soil – and they each came forth.
His voice thunders, roars, like a mighty waterfall;
All who hear this should tremble, and before Him fall.

He spoke, and birds, fishes, plants and animals came to life;
But when He made Adam and His wife,
God formed Adam from the ground, Eve from His rib;
He breathed silently; Adam and Eve lived.

On Sinai's Mount, His majestic voice was heard;
He was so mighty, all the people feared.
Sin would be punished, He declared;
Those who obeyed His Word would be spared.

But when Elijah was sore distressed,
Some would even say deeply depressed,
God did not shout nor roar in voice;
Still and small was then His choice.

Now, no longer through prophets He speaks,
Nor through priests on mountain peaks.
When the right time had fully come,
God sent forth His only Son.

He became the Living Word
Through whom God's voice was to be heard.
In deeds of love and small creations,
He declared forgiveness to people of all nations,

Who will repent of their waywardness,
And seek to live in righteousness,
Trusting in His redeeming work on the cross,
Counting all else in this life but dross.

One day His voice will go forth as trumpet's sound,
And all His saints will leave the ground,
To fly to His glorious home on high,

Where there will be neither tear nor sigh.

We'll be forever with the Lord,
Who is th'eternal, Living Word;
In His presence we will then rejoice,
Listening to His sweet, gentle voice.

2 October 2012

PERSONAL MOMENTS

This was written while I was still living and working in the city of Chicago.

GOD'S SUNSHINE

I smile and sing all the day
Because the sun casts its bright ray
Down from the Heavens above,
To remind me of God's great love.
It shines upon this dark city,
Removing all clouds of self-pity.
Here and there, it seeps through windows,
Making bright the flowering rose.

It whispers gently to your heart,
And God's sweet peace it does impart.
As it peeks o'er the window sill,
It reminds us that God is still
In Heaven giving peace and joy
To every man, woman, girl or boy
Who to Him will give their all,
Whether it be great or small.

Even though this sun warms the heart,
Another Son does a greater part.
He lifts it up and holds it high
And keeps it for th'eternal Sky.
So why not let this Son come in
To cleanse your heart from all its sin?
To make it free, and happy too.
That's what this Son will do for you.

20 February 1957

BECAUSE HE FIRST LOVED ME

I love my Redeemer;
To think that He would die for me
Causes me to bow and pray to
The Lamb of Calvary.
I love my blessed Saviour
Because He first loved me.

I love the Son of God;
He is so lovely, pure and kind.
Because He is pure, He cleanses me
In body, soul and mind.
I love my blessed Saviour
Because He first loved me.

I love Christ my Saviour
Because He made my life anew;
He put within my heart a light,
And nothing, now, looks blue.
I love my blessed Saviour
Because He first loved me.

He put within my heart a song,
Which I sing now for thee;
It is the same sweet, happy song
I'll sing for eternity.
I love my blessed Saviour
Because He first loved me.

27 August 1957

While I was still single, which I was until the age of 32, I had about given up on the thought that I might ever be married. So I surrendered the matter of earthly love to the Lord. This is expressed in the following poem.

EARTHLY LOVE SURRENDERED

My earthly love I gave to Thee,
Believing someday it would be restored.
With whom, and when and where
I could not know nor have a care,
Because I trust my Jesus.

The space of seven years went by.
How oft' my yearning heart did cry
How long? How long? I'm so alone!
Does no one want me for his own?
I'm glad I have you Jesus.

My Heavenly Father said to me,
"Now seek my face, seek only Me."
My heart cried out, "I seek Thee, Lord.
Oh, please do lead me through Thy Word;
Let my life display my Jesus."

The Lord Himself is my delight;
To Him my hungry soul takes flight
And finds its great desire fulfilled:
Earth's love restored, heart's crying stilled.
Oh! Thank You Lord Jesus!

20 August 1970

IT GOES WITH THE SILVER HAIR

Once we were young and agile,
Now we're getting old and fragile.
We used to jump, run and sprint;
If we did that now, we'd need a splint
To protect the broken leg or arm;
We'd surely do ourselves some harm.

We took the stairs two at a time;
Now we little children must mime:
First left foot up one, then the right,
We struggle on with all our might.
When, at last, we reach the top,
Into the nearest chair we plop.

Please cut my meat for me, my Dear;
What did you say? I cannot hear
The fast speech or the mumble;
It all sounds like just a jumble
Of voice and intonation
Without any articulation.

I may not be so bad yet,
Only bordering on decrepit.
The brain's slowed down, but still works well.
Which car is mine, I still can tell.
Technology seems to have me beat,
But I can still email a treat!

6 August 2016

My youngest son, John Samuel Holt, was born 2 months early, and was diagnosed as having Down's syndrome. When I heard the news, I wept convulsively for a full hour, until my husband's words that he had heard from the Lord brought a measure of comfort. He shared with me that this was God's way of showing His love to us.

A few days later, God spoke to me through Psalm 126:5 – 6: "They that sow in tears shall reap in joy. He that goeth forth and weepeth, bearing precious seed, shall doubtless come again with rejoicing, bringing his sheaves with him." The promise He gave me was that, no matter how many tears we would have to shed, and how much effort we would have to put into it, John would be educable.

It took me a few months though, to come to an understanding of the truth that God was showing us His love by giving us this special child.

At the age of 37, John tragically died during an epileptic fit. A few months after John's sudden death, I wrote this next poem, which was both a means of expressing my grief, and of gaining a bit of closure.

WHEN SHALL I CEASE FOR YOU TO CRY?

My last-born thou, my first to die;
When shall I cease for you to cry?
Down's syndrome? NO! A tragedy!
I knew not how to care for thee.
But God, a promise gave to me;
This child to learn adept will be.

As an early babe, you couldn't awake
To drink enough milk your thirst to slake.
So desperately I prayed each day
For you to eat, not fade away.

Then on the day that you were due,
At once, awake, appetite you knew.

Another desperate battle when,
At three months, a chest infection
Laid you aside for three long weeks.
A mother for her baby weeps.
And God does hear her every prayer,
Keeping the infant in His care.

Your years of schooling went all right;
You learned to read, and then to write;
To swim, make friends, to tie your shoe;
God's promise that you'd learn came true.
You never were a boy to shirk;
At college you really learned to work.

At "Riverside" something went wrong:
You could no longer pray aloud.
And then you had a fit or two;
We knew not what came over you.
Only in Sheffield did we see
That you had, somehow, epilepsy.

Here in Farnborough, you worked with zeal,
Even though your pain was real.
We cut the drugs; welcome relief from pain;
Joy and freedom of speech you gained.
I'd feel so helpless when you had a fit;
You'd gasp for air and I'd wonder, "Is this it?"

The elders prayed for you at church,
That you no more with fits would lurch.
Each night I'd pray, "Please protect John,"
Until on that eventful one,
"My Lord, I leave him in Your hands."
He carried you to that joyful strand.

Instead of lifting from you "this thing,"
As Iain had prayed unto our King,
God lifted you from your shell of clay

To await the resurrection day –
When each other we'll see again;
We'll all be free from sorrow and pain.

Hallelujah!

23 May 2014

FOR THE RECENTLY BEREAVED

That Christ was born so long ago
Was evidence God loves us so.
You surely miss your late loved one;
God gave for us His only Son.

Whenever we so lonely feel,
God's love and grace are there to heal.
Jesus experienced all human woe
That He our every pain could know.

He bore it all upon the cross
When for our sins He bled and died.
Cry out to Him and you will find
True peace at His once-wounded side.

2014

I wrote this next poem in an attempt to bring some comfort to a young man I knew who had been turned down by the young lady he loved.

FOR THE BROKENHEARTED

What is unrequited love?
It is a pain, so hard to bear;
The one so hurt can barely move
His thoughts from the one who is so dear.

It cuts so deeply, like a knife,
Until one's appetite is gone.
All you want is joy in life;
Instead, each day is sad and long.

The one so hurt should have a fear
Lest he, himself, has failed to love
Some other one who holds him dear,
And tries so oft' that love to prove.

In filial* learn to be secure,
It is the first love that we know.
As we receive and give, for sure
Our strength to really love will grow.

Then when the lesson we have learned,
To care for others and to give
Ourselves unselfishly, we've earned
The privilege in love to live.

Agape** is the best of all:
It comes from God, immense and true.
When we in faith upon Him call,
He fills our hearts with this love, too.

The One who loved us most of all
Died on a cross, our souls to save.
Is it not time before Him to fall,

And to love Him, who Himself gave?

31 July 2012

"But God demonstrates His own love toward us, in that while we were still sinners, Christ died for us." Romans 5:8.

Jesus Christ said: "These things I command you, that you love one another." John 15:17.

* *Filial* is the Greek word for brotherly love.
** *Agape* is the Greek word for love that gives even if nothing is given in return. It is the love that God has for all humanity.

This poem was enclosed with a small, anonymous, Christmas gift to a homeless person sheltered by the Salvation Army.

TO A HOMELESS PERSON

Dear Friend,
I care enough to help you,
Although I am a stranger.
As we think of Jesus' birth,
His only cot a manger,
Let us think of why he came:
To rescue us all from danger.

He died upon a cruel cross
To pay our debt of sin;
He loves us so very much,
He came our love to win,
That we His glorious Home
Might also enter in.

6 December 2016

SONGS

Based on the hymn *Take the Name of Jesus With You*, by Lydia Baxter.
1809-1874.

TAKE THE NAME OF JESUS WITH YOU

Take the name of Jesus with you,
Child of God who wants to show
Men the Way of life and vict'ry;
Take it then wher'er you go.

Take the name of Jesus ever
To your friends and all you meet.
When temptations 'round them gather,
Lead them to the Saviour's feet.

Oh, the precious name of Jesus,
How it meets our every need
As we try to help our neighbour,
And the Spirit's leading heed!

At the name of Jesus bowing,
Men may find eternal life;
And the precious blood of Jesus
Meets their every need in life.

January 1965

Based on the hymn, *Jesus, I am Resting, Resting*, by Jean S. Pigott.
1845-1882.

JESUS, I AM WRESTLING, WRESTLING

1.   Jesus, I am wrestling, wrestling,
Wrestling in the Holy Ghost;
There's no other way to victory
'Gainst all Satan's host.
He would always try to tempt me,
And to keep me from Thy Word;
But I daily overcome him
By the Spirit's Sword.

*Jesus, I am wrestling, wrestling,
Wrestling in the Holy Ghost;
There's no other way to victory
'Gainst all Satan's host.*

2.   Jesus, all the powers of darkness
Would surround the heathen lands;
But, by wrestling on in prayer,
We'll break Satan's bands.
He would always keep the nations
From the knowledge of Thy love;
But, praise God! By prayer Thy power
Comes down from above.

Chorus

3.   Jesus, how shall those in bondage
Come into Thy liberty?
Help me wrestle on in prayer
To see victory.
Oh, to be an intercessor
Who knows how to persevere!
Come, subdue my human weakness;
This my daily prayer.

1966

To the American tune of *My Hope is Built on Nothing Less,* or, *Faith of Our Fathers.*

BECAUSE HE DIED UPON THE TREE

1. Because He died upon the tree,
    Eternal life is granted me.
    I was a sinner lost, undone,
    No-one could save but He alone.

    My Lord, Thou didst this all for me,
    That I from sin might be made free,
    That glory might be given to Thee.

2. My God in mercy looked on me,
    Opened my eyes; now I can see.
    I have no merit of my own;
    'Tis Jesus' blood that must atone.

    Chorus

3. By His great grace I am set free
    From sin, and death, and tyranny;
    The foe is conquered and undone.
    Now I am Christ's, and He's my own.

    Chorus

19 July 2009

CHRISTMAS

During the Christmas break of 1964, the British OM workers who were in England at that time all went to their own homes for the holiday. As an American I had no family here, so a lovely Christian family who lived in Walsall, near Birmingham, kindly invited me to spend the holidays with them. They had a son and daughter who were nearly the same age as I.

Their church had a thriving youth group, and every evening during that week in the run-up to Christmas, there was a fun get-together in one home or another, to which I was also welcomed. As I sat on the side of my bed that Christmas Eve, I took stock of the preceding days, the love and welcome I'd been shown made me reflect on that first Christmas where God, was also a visitor – to this earth – looking for a welcome. This poem expresses those thoughts.

WHAT IS CHRISTMAS FOR YOU?

With trees and bells and mistletoe
Each year we are accustomed so
At Christmas time to celebrate, and
No one could forget that date.
With manger scenes and stars so bright,
Remember we that holy night
When God came down to live with men,
That we might be His sons again.

He came to earth a humble way;
To instigate a holiday
Was not the plan He had in mind,
But rather, all lost men to find.
He did not come down to this earth
To merely fill men's hearts with mirth;
Repentance, rather, would He give,
That in Him we might ever live.

Now as we see the stars so bright,

May we remember, He's the Light
Of this dark world. When we behold
The manger scene, we may be bold
In giving thanks to God above,
Because He's proved to us His love.
So may this Christmas be for you
A day of worship through and through.

24 December 1964

Thoughts on Isaiah 9:2. "The people who walked in darkness have seen a great light; those who dwelt in the land of the shadow of death, upon them a light has shined."

THAT GREAT LIGHT

"The people that walked in darkness have seen a great light."
The promised Saviour dispels the darkness of our night.
'Tis for Him, the mighty Creator of all good things,
That church bells ring, and the choir sings.

As we remember the humble birth
Of the King of glory when He came to earth,
Think, too, that baby Jesus grew to be a strong
Man; the only One without sin.
So He was able to bear all our wrong,
And let His light shine in
To our lives, and forgive us all,
If in repentance and faith we before Him fall.

10 December 2017

THE COMINGS OF OUR KING

Throughout the ages, the writers foretold
Of a coming King in words so clear and bold.
His heel would be bruised; crushed, the serpent's head;
At His first advent, His blood would be shed.

The Seed of David was also God's Branch,
The Righteous One, Satan's power to stanch.
The Everlasting Father, the Prince of Peace
Who came to earth prisoners to release.

Though in a barn born, in a manger slept;
He was by God from every danger kept.
Bright angels announced His birth on the hills
To shepherds, whose hearts were so filled with thrills.

They told the glad news everywhere they went,
That God His Son to our dark world had sent.
Wise men came from lands that were very far,
Seeking the baby King, led by a star.

Jerusalem's people did not know Him
Except for Anna and old Simeon.
His very own people rejected Him
Who had come to release us all from sin.

On Calvary's tree He laid down His life;
Then picked it up again – He is alive!
Some day He will return, of kings the King,
Of lords the Lord, whose praises all shall sing.

7 November 2014

FURTHER PUBLICATIONS BY BETTY HOLT

The Deity of Jesus Christ

Thy Word is Truth

From Chicago to the Ends of the Earth

Roses, Marys & Others

Rosas, Marías & Otras

What Kind of Fruit Are We Bearing?

Praying to the Living God

Printed in Great Britain
by Amazon